# The Story of Camilla

# The Queen Who Won Over the World

### Son M. Fredrik

Copyright © 2025 by Son M. Fredrik

All rights reserved.

No part of this publication may be reproduced, distributed, or transmitted in any form order by any means, including photocopying, recording, or other electronic or mechanical methods, without the prior written permission of the publisher, except in the case of brief quotations embodied in critical reviews and certain other noncommercial uses permitted by copyright law.

# Table of content

Chapter 1.................................................................................5
  Early Life and Personal Foundations...........................................5
Chapter 2...............................................................................13
  The Love Story That Changed the Monarchy.........................13
    Early Love: A Royal Romance Begins................................. 14
    The Reignited Romance: Scandal, Scrutiny, and Separation... 16
    A Cornerstone of Camilla's Role in the Monarchy................ 21
Chapter 3...............................................................................24
  Duchess of Cornwall – Embracing Royal Life.......................... 24
    The Transition to Royal Life: A New Beginning.....................25
    Championing Causes: A Tireless Advocate for Change....... 28
    Reshaping Her Image: From Scandal to Respect.................31
    A Cornerstone of the Monarchy's Future............................. 33
Chapter 4...............................................................................36
  From Duchess to Queen Consort – The Road to the Throne...36
    A Historic Moment: The Passing of Queen Elizabeth II........ 37
    The Challenges of Stepping into a Role So Rich in Tradition 39
    Approaching the Role with Grace, Humility, and Personal Flair 42
    A Modern Queen Consort..................................................... 45
Chapter 5...............................................................................48
  Fashion as Power – The Queen Consort's Style Evolution...... 48
    Fashion as a Tool of Diplomacy and Tradition...................... 49

    From Understated Elegance to Bold Designer Pieces..........52

    Camilla's Legacy as a Fashion Icon........................................58

Chapter 6........................................................................................61

    Key Moments and Milestones – Camilla in the Spotlight..........61

        Blending Tradition with Modernity: A Queen Consort for the 21st Century................................................................................62

        Hillsborough Castle: A Moment of Public Transformation.....64

        The Impact of Camilla's Role at Home and Abroad..............70

        Legacy of Camilla in the Spotlight..........................................71

Chapter 7........................................................................................73

    Camilla's Philanthropy and Advocacy........................................73

        A Passion for Literacy and the Power of Reading.................74

        Supporting Victims of Domestic Abuse.................................77

        Camilla's Partnerships with Charitable Organizations.......... 80

        Personal Stories and Reflections from Her Charity Work..... 82

        Legacy of Camilla's Advocacy................................................84

Chapter 8........................................................................................86

    Her Influence on the Royal Family............................................. 86

        Camilla's Relationship with King Charles III: A Shared Journey................................................................................... 87

        Shaping the Modern Monarchy: Camilla's Subtle Influence..90

        Camilla's Role in Royal Events: A Subtle Shift in the Monarchy's Image................................................................... 93

        A Subtle but Lasting Impact................................................... 96

Chapter 9........................................................................................98

- The Media and Public Perception – The Queen Who Won Over the World .................................................................................. 98
  - From Tabloid Scrutiny to Public Redemption ........................ 99
  - Navigating Media Relations: A Delicate Balance ................ 102
  - The Role of Charity Work in Shaping Her Image ................ 105
  - The Careful Balance of Privacy and Public Duty ................ 107
  - The Queen Who Won Over the World ................................ 109
- Chapter 10 .................................................................................. 112
  - Camilla's Legacy .................................................................... 112
    - The Impact of Her Reign on Future Generations ................ 113
    - Reflections on Her Contributions to the Monarchy and British Society .................................................................................. 116
    - Speculations on How History Will Remember Queen Camilla .. 120
- Conclusion ................................................................................. 123

# Chapter 1

# Early Life and Personal Foundations

Queen Camilla's story begins in the heart of London, where she was born Camilla Rosemary Shand on July 17, 1947, into an aristocratic family with deep ties to the British upper class. Her father, Bruce Shand, was a decorated officer in the British Army and later became the chairman of a successful wine business. Her mother, Rosalind, was the daughter of a distinguished family with connections to both the peerage and the world of business. The Shand family, with their privileged position in society, provided Camilla with a life of opportunity and connection to Britain's elite circles.

Growing up in the countryside of East Sussex, Camilla's childhood was marked by a sense of both comfort and privilege. Her family's estate, shared with her two siblings, fostered a love of the outdoors, where long walks and equestrian pursuits became formative aspects of her early life. Her upbringing was grounded in the values of traditional British society, which, though protective, also exposed her to the complex social codes and expectations of aristocracy. This world, so familiar to her, would serve her later as she navigated the more public aspects of royal life.

Her education played an integral role in shaping the woman she would become. Camilla attended the prestigious Queens Gate School in London and later went on to study at the finishing school in Switzerland, where she honed skills that would later make her an invaluable member of the royal family. Her time at school was not just about academics; it was a training ground for diplomacy and public decorum. As with most children in the upper echelons of British society, she was taught the importance of social grace, manners, and the ability to handle both public scrutiny and private matters with composure. This education laid the groundwork for the strong will, wit, and emotional intelligence that Camilla would later exhibit in her royal duties.

Despite being raised in an environment where expectations were high, Camilla was known for her down-to-earth, approachable personality. An anecdote often told about her childhood speaks to this: on a family trip to Spain, a young Camilla made a particularly striking impression when she casually sat down next to a famous royal guest at a dinner party. The guest, initially taken aback by her lack of pretense, later recalled how she charmed him with her wit and lack of artifice. Even in her younger years, it was clear that Camilla had a natural ability to make others feel comfortable, an asset that would later become invaluable in her royal life. Her charm was never the result of calculated effort but an authentic extension of her personality.

Her personality was shaped by the values imparted to her by her parents: integrity, social responsibility, and a deep sense of duty. However, it was her love for literature and the arts that set her apart from many of her peers. Camilla was an avid reader, known for her sharp intellect and insightful observations. Whether discussing poetry, history, or contemporary affairs, she possessed the ability to engage in conversations on a wide range of topics, demonstrating the kind of wit and intellectual curiosity that would eventually earn her admiration within royal circles.

Though often shy and reserved in her early years, there was an undeniable strength to her character. This was a woman who was already beginning to understand the demands of public life, even before she would ever formally step into the spotlight. The early signs of someone capable of balancing personal relationships with public duties were evident from a young age. She had already begun to develop a deep understanding of the expectations that would one day accompany her as a member of the royal family.

One pivotal moment in her early life that shaped her future was her decision to embrace the role of a hostess and caretaker in her family's home. The Shand estate was often a hub for social gatherings, and Camilla quickly became known for her warmth and hospitality. This ability to create a welcoming environment and foster genuine connections with a wide array of people would prove to be one of her greatest assets when she later entered the royal family, where such qualities were essential to her work.

Camilla's early life was not without its challenges. A brief engagement to the charismatic Andrew Parker Bowles in the 1970s was, in hindsight, a foreshadowing of the complicated relationships that would play a role in her life, particularly her relationship with Prince Charles. Despite the ups and downs, these formative years were a period of personal growth, where she developed the inner fortitude and understanding that would allow her to navigate the complexities of her later life in the public eye. Through all the transitions, Camilla's genuine nature never wavered, and it was this authenticity that would ultimately resonate with those around her.

The woman who would one day become Queen Consort was already beginning to emerge during these early years. The foundation of her strong character, rooted in a life of privilege, education, and personal experiences, had already been set. Little did the world know that these early signs of warmth, wit, and understanding would evolve into the qualities that would help her play a pivotal role in one of the world's most revered institutions—the British monarchy.

# Chapter 2

# The Love Story That Changed the Monarchy

The love story between Camilla Shand and Prince Charles is one of the most passionate and complex relationships in modern royal history. Their journey, which spanned decades and was fraught with public scandal, media scrutiny, and personal challenges, ultimately became a defining element of their lives. This chapter delves into the intricacies of their relationship, from their early love to the tumultuous years that followed, shedding light on how their bond, despite numerous obstacles, became a cornerstone of Camilla's future role within the British monarchy.

## Early Love: A Royal Romance Begins

Their story began in the early 1970s, when Camilla Shand and Prince Charles first met through mutual friends at a polo match. At the time, Camilla was a young, vivacious woman from an aristocratic family, and Charles, the heir to the British throne, was in his early twenties. Despite their differences in title, the two shared a connection that seemed almost immediate. It was a relationship rooted in a shared love of the outdoors, intellectual conversation, and an understanding of one another's world. For Charles, Camilla was unlike anyone he had met before—outspoken, independent, and unapologetically herself. For Camilla, the Prince was charming but also burdened with the weight of royal expectations, something she understood through her own experiences in the aristocracy.

Their connection quickly blossomed into a romantic relationship. Charles was captivated by Camilla's intelligence and free-spirited nature, while she appreciated his depth and sense of duty. However, their romance was not to be. In 1973, Camilla became engaged to Andrew Parker Bowles, a charming army officer, and Charles, under pressure from the royal family, was encouraged to marry someone who could fulfill the public expectations of a future Queen consort.

Despite their separation, both Charles and Camilla remained fond of each other. Their paths diverged for many years, but their bond, never fully extinguished, lingered in the background. The love between them, though initially sidelined by circumstances, was never truly forgotten. Camilla, now married and with children, continued her life while Charles, though romantically linked to others, was deeply affected by the memory of her.

## The Reignited Romance: Scandal, Scrutiny, and Separation

As both Camilla and Prince Charles grew older, their lives began to intertwine once more. Camilla's marriage to Andrew Parker Bowles ended in divorce in 1995, and Charles, too, faced difficulties in his marriage to Princess Diana. The breakdown of Charles's marriage, alongside the growing media fascination with his relationship with Diana, created a storm of controversy. Public opinion was divided, and the press, eager to capture every scandalous detail, focused their attention on Camilla, often portraying her as the villain in the royal love triangle.

The late 1990s marked a turning point. The once quiet and private affair between Camilla and Charles was thrust into the public eye, and their relationship was dissected in the tabloids. The press painted Camilla as the "other woman," a label that stuck for years. However, the reality of their partnership was more complicated than the tabloid narratives suggested.

Despite the intense media scrutiny, Camilla stood by Charles, their bond growing even stronger in the face of public adversity.

During this period, both Charles and Camilla suffered from the weight of public judgment. Their personal lives were no longer private, and every move they made was scrutinized. Camilla's reputation, already tarnished by her past involvement with Charles, became further vilified by the press. She became a scapegoat for the public's disillusionment with the royal family, especially following Princess Diana's tragic death in 1997. Yet, through it all, Charles and Camilla's relationship endured. Their reunion was a testament to the depth of their affection for one another.

The Turning Point: A Public Acknowledgment and the Road to Marriage

The year 2005 marked a turning point in their relationship. After years of secrecy, scandal, and public condemnation, Charles and Camilla finally made the decision to marry. Their wedding, which took place on April 9, 2005, was a quieter affair compared to other royal weddings, but its significance was immense. For the first time, Camilla was officially recognized as Prince Charles's partner in a legal and ceremonial sense.

The public reaction to their marriage was mixed, with some still harboring negative views of Camilla due to her role in Charles and Diana's marriage breakdown.

However, over time, public sentiment shifted. Camilla's dignity, grace, and sense of duty began to shine through. As she took on royal duties alongside Charles, she showed a willingness to embrace her role with humility and commitment, slowly winning the approval of those who had once viewed her with skepticism.

This chapter in their story not only marked the end of years of public scrutiny but also marked the beginning of a new era for both Camilla and Charles. While their relationship was controversial, it had weathered the storms of public opinion, scandal, and personal heartbreak. Through it all, their love had only deepened, and they were able to finally share their lives together openly, without the cloud of secrecy that had once hovered over them.

## A Cornerstone of Camilla's Role in the Monarchy

Charles and Camilla's relationship, rocky at times and fraught with complications, ultimately laid the foundation for Camilla's future role within the monarchy. Their partnership proved to be a vital cornerstone of her life as Queen Consort. As Prince Charles ascended to the throne, Camilla assumed a role that was both public and private, one that required her to balance her personal history with the duties expected of her as consort to the King.

Her transition from a figure who was once vilified to one who would play a vital role in the future of the British monarchy is a testament to her resilience and strength. Camilla's relationship with Charles, built on years of understanding, respect, and affection, would not only define her life but would also be an essential element in the shaping of the modern monarchy.

Their love story, once filled with scandal and controversy, became a model of enduring affection and commitment. It was a tale that changed the monarchy, setting the stage for a new era of public relations, royal duties, and personal relationships within the royal family. Their story, with all its complexities, has left an indelible mark on history, one that continues to shape Camilla's role as Queen Consort.

# Chapter 3

# Duchess of Cornwall – Embracing Royal Life

The transition from Camilla Shand, a private individual, to the Duchess of Cornwall, a title she would hold for the majority of her life before becoming Queen Consort, was not an easy one. The shift marked a pivotal moment in her personal journey and in her role within the royal family. The world watched as she adapted to the demands of public life, took on royal duties, and became a prominent figure in British society. This chapter delves into Camilla's early years as Duchess, highlighting her charity work, her steadfast commitment to important causes, and the gradual shift in public perception that would shape her legacy as one of the monarchy's most respected figures.

## The Transition to Royal Life: A New Beginning

When Camilla married Prince Charles in 2005, she knew that her life would change irrevocably. No longer just the woman behind the scenes, Camilla had to step into the public eye in a way she never had before. As Duchess of Cornwall, her responsibilities now extended far beyond her private life. She was expected to fulfill numerous ceremonial duties, attend state functions, and represent the royal family in various capacities both in the UK and abroad. It was a challenging transition—one that involved both personal sacrifice and public scrutiny.

Her role as Duchess required her to balance royal protocol with her own distinct personality. Unlike her predecessors, Camilla was not a born princess, and she did not come from a background steeped in royal tradition. However, her upbringing in an aristocratic family had prepared her well for life in the public eye. The confidence and grace with which she approached her new role quickly became apparent to those around her. She was not merely performing ceremonial tasks; she was taking on a leadership role, one that would eventually allow her to carve out her own space in the royal family.

Despite her readiness to embrace this new chapter, Camilla's transition was not without challenges. The press had not fully accepted her as the rightful partner of the heir to the throne, and many in the public remained wary of her due to her earlier relationship with Prince Charles and the public fallout from his marriage to Princess Diana. However, Camilla approached these challenges with an unyielding sense of duty and perseverance. Her sincerity and commitment to her new role were undeniable, and over time, the public began to see the depth of her devotion to the responsibilities of her title.

# Championing Causes: A Tireless Advocate for Change

From the very beginning of her role as Duchess of Cornwall, Camilla demonstrated an unwavering commitment to charitable causes. One of her first and most important initiatives was her involvement with literacy programs, which became a defining focus of her charitable work. As someone who deeply valued education, she worked tirelessly to promote reading and literacy, particularly for disadvantaged children. Her efforts included working with organizations like the National Literacy Trust, which aimed to improve literacy rates and provide access to books and educational resources in underprivileged communities.

Camilla's involvement with causes close to her heart went beyond just literacy. She became an outspoken advocate for domestic violence victims, bringing attention to the often-overlooked issue and working with various organizations to provide support and resources for those affected. Her work in this area was not just ceremonial; she met with victims, listened to their stories, and helped raise awareness of the prevalence of domestic violence across the UK.

In addition to her work with domestic violence and literacy, Camilla also became involved in cancer research, supporting initiatives aimed at improving the lives of those affected by the disease. She played an instrumental role in raising funds for cancer research and advocating for early detection, helping to ensure that cancer patients received the care and support they needed. Through her involvement with a wide range of charities, Camilla began to solidify her reputation as a compassionate, tireless advocate for change.

Her work was not without challenges, however. While Camilla was dedicated to these causes, she also had to contend with skepticism from the public. Many people viewed her as the woman who had disrupted the royal family's image and was unfairly blamed for the breakdown of Charles's marriage to Diana. But Camilla's actions spoke louder than words. Her willingness to take on causes that others might shy away from, coupled with her genuine compassion, slowly earned her respect in the eyes of the public.

## Reshaping Her Image: From Scandal to Respect

One of the most remarkable aspects of Camilla's role as Duchess of Cornwall was her ability to overcome the public's skepticism and reshaping her image from that of the "other woman" to a respected member of the royal family. Early in her marriage to Charles, she was the subject of intense media scrutiny. The press continued to label her as the "villain" of the royal story, a woman who had been at the center of Charles's troubled marriage to Princess Diana.

Despite this, Camilla handled the intense media coverage with remarkable poise. She remained calm in the face of criticism, focusing on her royal duties and charitable work rather than engaging in the public drama that surrounded her. Slowly but surely, she began to turn the tide of public opinion. Her consistency in supporting important causes and her genuine, down-to-earth nature won over many of the British public, who saw in her a woman who was both capable and compassionate.

Camilla's tireless commitment to her duties, along with her ability to adapt to the royal life, contributed to a significant shift in her image. The public began to see her not as the woman who had caused royal scandal, but as a figure who was devoted to service, dignity, and responsibility. By the time Prince Charles ascended to the throne in 2022, Camilla was not only accepted by the public but was also admired for the role she had played in modernizing the monarchy and supporting her husband during one of the most important transitions in British history.

## A Cornerstone of the Monarchy's Future

By the time Camilla assumed the role of Queen Consort, she had fully embraced her position within the royal family. Her journey from the Duchess of Cornwall to Queen Consort was not merely a change in title—it was a testament to the strength of her character, the depth of her commitment to the monarchy, and the respect she had earned through years of service. Her work with charities, her ability to navigate public scrutiny, and her unwavering support for her husband, King Charles III, helped lay the groundwork for her future role as Queen Consort.

As Duchess of Cornwall, Camilla proved that she was more than just a royal by marriage. She became a vital part of the royal family, a woman whose contributions to society and to the monarchy were immeasurable. Through her charitable work, her dedication to royal duties, and her ability to reshape public perception, Camilla cemented her place as one of the most respected members of the British royal family. And, as she stepped into the role of Queen Consort, her legacy as the Duchess of Cornwall remained an essential part of her story—a story of perseverance, growth, and unwavering dedication to service.

# Chapter 4

## From Duchess to Queen Consort – The Road to the Throne

The transition from the Duchess of Cornwall to Queen Consort was a monumental and historic moment in the life of Camilla. It marked the culmination of years of public scrutiny, personal growth, and the gradual reshaping of her image within the royal family. As the wife of Prince Charles, who ascended to the throne as King Charles III following the death of Queen Elizabeth II, Camilla found herself in a new role that demanded both sensitivity and strength. This chapter delves into the emotional and historic moment when

Camilla became Queen Consort, the challenges she faced in stepping into a role so rich in tradition, and the grace and humility with which she approached this significant change in her life and royal duties.

## A Historic Moment: The Passing of Queen Elizabeth II

The passing of Queen Elizabeth II on September 8, 2022, marked the end of a 70-year reign, ushering in a new era for the British monarchy. As the longest-reigning monarch in British history, Queen Elizabeth II had set an unshakable precedent for what it meant to be a monarch, and the expectations surrounding her successor were immense. Her death was not only a personal loss for her family but also a defining moment in the history of the United Kingdom and the Commonwealth.

For Camilla, the moment was deeply emotional. As the wife of Prince Charles, she had stood by him throughout their years of marriage, but now, she was facing a vastly different reality. The title of Queen Consort, while one she had long anticipated in the back of her mind, was now hers to bear. The passing of Queen Elizabeth II meant that Charles was no longer just the Prince of Wales; he was now the King, and Camilla's role as his wife would evolve from that of a supportive partner to the official consort of a reigning monarch.

Though Camilla had been preparing for this moment in a public sense for many years, the weight of her new role still carried immense significance. In the days and weeks following the Queen's death, the royal family was thrust into a period of mourning and transition. The eyes of the world were on Camilla, as the new Queen Consort, to see how she would handle this shift in responsibility and public perception.

## The Challenges of Stepping into a Role So Rich in Tradition

Becoming Queen Consort was not just a change in title for Camilla; it was a monumental shift in her public role, one that came with the weight of centuries of tradition. The position of Queen Consort has historically been filled by women who, in many ways, have been expected to serve as symbols of national unity, duty, and grace. It was a role steeped in royal protocol, one that required a careful balance of personal identity and public duty.

For Camilla, the challenges of stepping into such a prestigious role were evident. Though she had already served as a supportive and active member of the royal family during her years as the Duchess of Cornwall, being Queen Consort came with additional pressures. She was now the wife of the reigning King, a role that placed her in the public spotlight in a way she had never experienced before.

Perhaps the greatest challenge Camilla faced was overcoming the lingering public perception that had followed her for decades. For years, she had been the subject of tabloid speculation and criticism, particularly due to her involvement in the breakdown of Prince Charles's marriage to Princess Diana. Though public opinion had softened over the years as Camilla had proven her commitment to royal duties and charitable causes, there was still a segment of the public that viewed her with skepticism.

Additionally, the legacy of Queen Elizabeth II loomed large. Queen Elizabeth had been a steadfast figurehead, universally admired for her unwavering dedication to the monarchy and her role as a symbol of continuity. Camilla's ascension to Queen Consort came at a time when the monarchy itself was undergoing scrutiny and was in need of modernization. The royal family, and particularly Camilla, had to navigate these shifting dynamics while respecting the legacy of Queen Elizabeth II.

# Approaching the Role with Grace, Humility, and Personal Flair

Despite the immense challenges, Camilla approached her new role with a combination of grace, humility, and personal flair that would come to define her as Queen Consort. Rather than attempt to fill the shoes of Queen Elizabeth II, Camilla sought to carve out her own identity within the monarchy, drawing on the lessons she had learned during her years as the Duchess of Cornwall.

Camilla's natural warmth, approachability, and wit quickly became assets in her new role. She had already earned the respect of many in the royal family and among the British public through her charitable work, her steady presence at royal events, and her genuine concern for the well-being of others. As Queen Consort, these qualities would continue to serve her well as she worked to represent the King and the monarchy.

One of the first public appearances Camilla made as Queen Consort was during the official mourning period for Queen Elizabeth II. At this time, Camilla demonstrated a quiet dignity and composure that resonated with both the public and the media. Rather than seeking the limelight, she supported her husband, King Charles III, and participated in key ceremonial events with a sense of reverence and respect for the traditions of the monarchy.

Her ability to navigate the complex dynamics of the royal family and the public spotlight with tact and humility allowed her to gradually earn the trust and admiration of those who had once been skeptical of her role. Camilla's natural elegance and personal charm became defining traits of her reign as Queen Consort, and she soon established herself as an indispensable partner to King Charles III.

Perhaps most notably, Camilla did not seek to overshadow the legacy of Queen Elizabeth II but instead built on it. She embraced her new responsibilities with a sense of purpose and a clear understanding of the weight of history, while simultaneously adding her own distinctive touch. Whether attending state functions, hosting events at Buckingham Palace, or participating in charity work, Camilla brought her unique warmth and authenticity to the role.

## A Modern Queen Consort

Camilla's ascension to the throne as Queen Consort was not just the fulfillment of a long-held title; it was a moment of transformation for the monarchy itself. In her new role, she became a symbol of continuity and modernity—respecting the rich traditions of the British royal family while also ushering in a new era. Through her resilience, humility, and distinctive personal style, Camilla proved herself to be not just a supportive partner to King Charles III, but an essential figure in the monarchy's future.

In the face of immense pressure, Camilla approached her new role with the same steady determination that had defined her years as the Duchess of Cornwall. Her journey from a controversial figure to a beloved Queen Consort is a testament to her strength, grace, and unwavering commitment to public service. The road to the throne was not without its challenges, but Camilla's quiet resolve and ability to balance tradition with personal authenticity ensured that her place in history was firmly secured.

As Queen Consort, Camilla's influence within the royal family will continue to evolve. She has proven that, while the monarchy may be steeped in history, it can also be adaptable to the changing times. Her journey to the throne is one of personal growth, resilience, and the quiet strength that has always defined her. And as she steps into this new chapter, she is not just the wife of King Charles III; she is a modern monarch in her own right, a Queen Consort whose legacy will be remembered for generations to come.

# Chapter 5

# Fashion as Power – The Queen Consort's Style Evolution

Fashion has always been more than just a reflection of personal taste; for Queen Camilla, it has served as a powerful tool of diplomacy, self-expression, and tradition. As she transitioned from the Duchess of Cornwall to Queen Consort, her wardrobe became a key element of her public persona. Each choice, from understated elegance to bold designer pieces, reflected her journey within the monarchy, her growing confidence, and her desire to balance modernity with royal tradition. This chapter delves into Camilla's style evolution, examining how her fashion choices tell a story of personal growth, her relationship with iconic designers, and the way her wardrobe has become an extension of her royal persona.

# Fashion as a Tool of Diplomacy and Tradition

From the moment Camilla stepped into the royal spotlight, her wardrobe became a vehicle for communicating more than just personal style—it was a method of representing the monarchy. As the Duchess of Cornwall, she often used fashion to convey respect for the traditions of the royal family, while subtly infusing her own identity into her attire. When she ascended to the role of Queen Consort, her fashion choices became even more significant, signaling her understanding of the symbolic weight of her position.

For Camilla, dressing for royal engagements meant embracing both tradition and diplomacy. She often wore outfits that adhered to the established royal dress codes, with tailored suits, modest hemlines, and restrained color palettes. Yet, even within the confines of royal protocol, her fashion choices were never stiff or predictable. Instead, they conveyed a sense of quiet authority and confidence, which was particularly evident during official engagements and state functions.

Her appearance at Hillsborough Castle in Northern Ireland in 2023 is a prime example of Camilla's ability to use fashion as a diplomatic tool. At the event, she wore a beautifully tailored spring outfit that was both elegant and understated, with a subtle nod to her style evolution. The look, which included a muted floral dress paired with a smart jacket and accessories, communicated a sense of respect for the event's significance while still allowing her to shine as a modern queen. The outfit conveyed warmth and approachability, qualities that have become trademarks of her royal presence.

Her fashion choices at such high-profile events are a reminder that, in the royal family, what is worn is never just about the garment itself. Every outfit is a reflection of the monarchy's values, the royal family's role in the world, and the Queen Consort's personal identity. Camilla's wardrobe is a constant balancing act—respecting tradition, representing the monarchy, and expressing her individuality, all while staying true to the values of the royal family.

## From Understated Elegance to Bold Designer Pieces

Camilla's style has undergone a remarkable transformation since she first appeared in the public eye. Early in her royal life, her fashion choices were often marked by an understated elegance. She favored classic cuts and simple, elegant colors that allowed her to blend into the background, fulfilling her royal duties without overshadowing other members of the family. This approach was in line with the expectations of a duchess, where her role was largely supportive and her fashion was functional.

However, as her confidence grew, so did her style. Camilla began to embrace more daring fashion choices, incorporating vibrant colors, statement accessories, and bold prints into her wardrobe. Her style evolved from simple, demure designs to more dynamic, fashion-forward outfits. This shift reflected her growing confidence and acceptance of her role within the royal family. She was no longer the Duchess of Cornwall simply supporting her husband; she was a key figure in the monarchy, a Queen Consort in the making, and her wardrobe reflected this transformation.

In her new role as Queen Consort, Camilla's fashion choices became a celebration of both personal taste and royal duty. She began incorporating pieces from high-end designers, making appearances in sleek, modern silhouettes that contrasted with the more traditional, formal attire expected of a royal consort. These bold fashion moments, often seen during state visits or formal gatherings, communicated a sense of authority and individuality. For instance, her attire at the 2023 State Banquet, which included a striking dress by a leading British designer, marked a significant shift in how she was perceived—no longer merely a consort, but a queen with her own voice and vision.

Her ability to combine classic royal style with a modern twist has become one of Camilla's signature traits. Whether she's wearing an intricately detailed gown at a royal function or a more relaxed ensemble during a charity event, her fashion choices consistently show a woman who is both grounded in tradition and unafraid to experiment with her look. This balance between tradition and modernity has made her a fashion icon in her own right, admired for her ability to stay true to herself while honoring the monarchy's legacy.

Camilla's Relationship with Designers: A Personal Touch

A key element of Camilla's style evolution has been her close relationship with select designers, particularly those who understand her personal taste and the unique challenges of dressing a Queen Consort. One of the most notable partnerships in her fashion journey has been with the iconic jewelry brand Van Cleef & Arpels. The brand's timeless, elegant pieces have become a staple of Camilla's wardrobe, adding a touch of sophistication and luxury to her public appearances.

Her affinity for Van Cleef & Arpels is not merely about wearing expensive jewelry—it's about making a statement of grace, history, and continuity. The jewelry pieces she wears often feature intricate designs that are rich in symbolism, reflecting both her personal story and her evolving role as Queen Consort. For example, the Van Cleef & Arpels earrings she wore during her visit to Hillsborough Castle became symbolic of her transformation as a royal figure. They were a nod to her refined taste, but also a subtle declaration that she was now a queen who would carry the weight of the monarchy with elegance and dignity.

Camilla's relationship with her designers goes beyond simple fashion choices. It is a collaboration built on mutual respect and understanding. She works closely with her designers to ensure that her outfits are not only beautiful but also appropriate for the duties she must fulfill. In many ways, her style has become a reflection of her relationship with the designers she works with—there is a clear understanding of what she needs as a queen, as well as a deep respect for her individuality as a woman.

For Camilla, jewelry has become much more than just an accessory. It has evolved into an integral part of her royal persona. From her understated pieces to her more statement-making designs, the jewelry she chooses speaks volumes about her position within the royal family and her personal journey. It is an extension of her character—a symbol of her elegance, strength, and sense of tradition.

## Camilla's Legacy as a Fashion Icon

As Queen Consort, Camilla has firmly established herself as a modern fashion icon. Her wardrobe is no longer just a tool for diplomatic duty—it is a reflection of her journey, her personal growth, and her increasing confidence in her role. From her early days as the Duchess of Cornwall, where she favored subtle elegance, to her later years as Queen Consort, where she embraced bold designs and statement pieces, Camilla's fashion has evolved in tandem with her own transformation within the monarchy.

Her relationship with designers, particularly with brands like Van Cleef & Arpels, has added a layer of sophistication and timelessness to her image. Jewelry, once a simple accessory, has become a signature part of her royal persona, adding depth and meaning to her style.

In the years to come, Camilla's style will likely continue to evolve, reflecting the changing times while honoring the traditions of the monarchy. But one thing is clear: her fashion choices have become a powerful tool of self-expression, a symbol of her place within the royal family, and a legacy in their own right. Her journey from the Duchess of Cornwall to Queen Consort has been reflected not only in her words and actions but in the clothes she wears and the way she carries herself.

# Chapter 6

# Key Moments and Milestones – Camilla in the Spotlight

As Queen Consort, Camilla has faced numerous pivotal moments that have shaped her reign and helped define her role within the monarchy. From state visits to royal ceremonies, each appearance has showcased her ability to seamlessly blend tradition with modernity, demonstrating her deep understanding of both her royal duties and the evolving nature of the monarchy. These moments not only highlight her growing confidence as Queen Consort but also reflect her natural diplomatic skills and ability to connect with people from all walks of life. This chapter delves into some of the key moments and milestones that have placed Camilla in the spotlight, including her appearance at Hillsborough Castle, a significant event in her royal journey.

## Blending Tradition with Modernity: A Queen Consort for the 21st Century

Camilla's reign as Queen Consort has been marked by her ability to maintain the traditions of the British monarchy while introducing a more modern and relatable approach. As the consort of King Charles III, she is not only tasked with upholding the legacy of the monarchy but also with ensuring it remains relevant in an increasingly fast-paced world. Throughout her public appearances, Camilla has demonstrated a skillful ability to honor royal protocol while embracing the modern expectations of transparency, approachability, and public engagement.

One of the key ways she has done this is through her consistent presence at both traditional royal events and contemporary engagements. Whether attending the state banquets of visiting dignitaries or participating in community outreach events, Camilla has proven her versatility. She can move effortlessly between formal, ceremonial occasions—where the weight of tradition is paramount—and more casual, modern engagements—where her warm and approachable nature shines through. This balance is essential for the monarchy's survival in the 21st century, and Camilla's ability to embody both tradition and modernity has made her an essential figure in the royal family.

## Hillsborough Castle: A Moment of Public Transformation

One of the most significant moments in Camilla's journey as Queen Consort occurred during her visit to Hillsborough Castle in Northern Ireland in 2023. The event, held to celebrate the official visit of King Charles III, was a key moment not only in her reign but also in her relationship with the public. Camilla's appearance at the event marked a shift in the public's perception of her, solidifying her image as a dignified, compassionate, and confident queen.

At Hillsborough Castle, Camilla donned a striking spring outfit—an elegant floral dress paired with a tailored jacket—along with exquisite jewelry from Van Cleef & Arpels, signaling her growing role as a fashion icon. But the impact of her presence went far beyond her attire. The event itself, which was marked by public and press attention, demonstrated Camilla's unique ability to command the spotlight while exuding warmth and authenticity.

In many ways, the Hillsborough Castle event was symbolic of Camilla's evolving role as Queen Consort. While she had long been a royal figure, her status had often been questioned due to her past. Yet at this event, the public and media witnessed a Camilla who had fully embraced her royal duties. She was no longer seen as an outsider or a controversial figure but as a queen in her own right—one who understood the responsibilities of her position and who had earned her place beside King Charles III.

The event also highlighted Camilla's growing confidence as she interacted with the public, showcasing her ability to connect with people in a genuine and personable way. Her poised yet approachable demeanor made her accessible to the people she serves, reinforcing the idea that the monarchy is not just a distant institution but one that is deeply connected to the people of the United Kingdom.

Diplomatic Roles and Interactions with Global Leaders

One of the most vital aspects of Camilla's role as Queen Consort has been her diplomatic work. As the wife of King Charles III, she has often represented the monarchy on the international stage, accompanying him on state visits and meeting with world leaders. Through these diplomatic engagements, Camilla has played an integral role in strengthening the UK's global relationships and enhancing the monarchy's international presence.

Her interactions with global leaders, from heads of state to cultural ambassadors, have consistently shown her to be a competent and effective representative of the British monarchy. Camilla's natural grace and diplomatic skills have earned her the respect of foreign dignitaries, while her ability to engage in meaningful conversations has made her a welcomed figure at international events.

During her state visit to Germany alongside King Charles, Camilla was praised for her warm and approachable demeanor. In her interactions with German President Frank-Walter Steinmeier and Chancellor Olaf Scholz, she exuded a calm authority while also embracing moments of lightheartedness. These interactions showcased her ability to adapt to different cultural settings while representing British values with elegance.

On state visits to the Commonwealth, Camilla has similarly used her role to foster goodwill and strengthen ties with former colonies. Her visits to

Australia and Canada, for example, demonstrated her deep commitment to maintaining the monarchy's relevance in the modern world while respecting the diverse histories and cultures of these nations.

Her diplomatic work also extends to her role as a patron of various charitable organizations. In meeting with international leaders, Camilla often advocates for issues that are important to her, such as literacy, domestic violence, and women's rights. These engagements highlight her commitment to using her platform as Queen Consort to promote causes that align with the values of the monarchy while improving the lives of people across the globe.

# The Impact of Camilla's Role at Home and Abroad

Camilla's diplomatic and public roles serve to remind the world that the monarchy is an institution that transcends borders. Her work abroad has allowed the monarchy to maintain its relevance on the global stage, demonstrating that it is not only concerned with British affairs but also with fostering relationships that benefit the UK and the Commonwealth.

At home, Camilla continues to be a steady and stabilizing presence within the royal family. Her commitment to charitable causes, her tireless support of King Charles III, and her involvement in royal engagements have cemented her status as a key figure in the British monarchy. In addition to her formal duties, Camilla has become a trusted and respected member of the royal family, one whose actions and decisions are followed closely by both the British public and the global media.

Through her diplomatic work and her engagement with global leaders, Camilla has proven that she is not just a Queen Consort in title but a Queen Consort in action. Her ability to balance the demands of royal life with the expectations of a modern monarch has made her an indispensable partner to King Charles III, and her presence at key moments continues to shape the future of the monarchy.

## Legacy of Camilla in the Spotlight

As Queen Consort, Camilla's legacy will undoubtedly be shaped by these key moments and milestones. From her transformative appearance at Hillsborough Castle to her diplomatic interactions with global leaders, Camilla has proven that she is a queen for the modern era—one who embodies both the grace of tradition and the dynamism of the present. Her ability to blend tradition with modernity, coupled with her commitment to public service and her diplomatic acumen, ensures that her place in history is one that will be remembered with respect and admiration.

# Chapter 7

# Camilla's Philanthropy and Advocacy

Camilla, Queen Consort of the United Kingdom, is not only known for her role within the royal family but also for her unwavering commitment to philanthropy and advocacy. Over the years, she has become one of the most dedicated champions of social causes within the royal family, focusing her efforts on issues such as literacy, domestic abuse, and community well-being. Her philanthropic work is not merely ceremonial; it is a deeply personal commitment that continues to make a significant impact on countless lives. This chapter takes a deeper dive into Camilla's charity work, exploring her longstanding involvement in these causes, her partnerships with key organizations, and how she continues to use her platform to bring attention to social issues.

## A Passion for Literacy and the Power of Reading

One of the most significant areas of Camilla's philanthropic focus has been literacy. As someone who values education deeply, she has worked tirelessly to support initiatives aimed at improving literacy rates across the United Kingdom, particularly for children and adults from disadvantaged backgrounds. In her role as the royal patron of the

National Literacy Trust, Camilla has been at the forefront of efforts to promote reading as a means of personal empowerment.

Her involvement in literacy initiatives is driven by her belief in the transformative power of reading. She often speaks about how books can offer individuals an escape, a source of learning, and a way to improve their quality of life. In her charity work, Camilla has not only supported national reading campaigns but has also visited schools, libraries, and reading programs across the UK, engaging directly with children and young adults to encourage a love for reading.

One of the flagship programs she has championed is the *Big Lunch*, an initiative designed to encourage communities to come together and celebrate food, friendship, and shared experiences. Though not solely focused on literacy, *The Big Lunch* serves as a platform for Camilla to highlight the importance of social connections and how literacy and education can play a pivotal role in strengthening communities. Through this initiative, Camilla has emphasized the value of collective effort, demonstrating that small acts of kindness—such as reading together or organizing a community gathering—can make a big difference in promoting education.

Camilla's passion for literacy is evident in her ongoing efforts to improve literacy levels and encourage lifelong learning. In her role as Queen Consort, she has continued to advocate for these causes, making sure that they remain at the forefront of her charitable work. She has often spoken about how education is not just about books but about shaping the minds and futures of young people, giving them the tools they need to succeed in life.

## Supporting Victims of Domestic Abuse

Another cause that Camilla has championed with great dedication is supporting victims of domestic abuse. She has long been an advocate for those who suffer in silence, and her work in this area has been both deeply personal and professional. As a patron of organizations like *SafeLives* and *Women's Aid*, Camilla has worked tirelessly to raise awareness of domestic violence and provide support for victims. Her role in bringing attention to the issue has been instrumental in ensuring that victims of abuse are given the help they need to rebuild their lives.

Camilla has spoken candidly about the importance of tackling the issue of domestic abuse head-on, highlighting that it remains one of the most significant social challenges facing families across the UK. Through her involvement in numerous campaigns and charity events, Camilla has helped to break the stigma surrounding domestic violence, providing a platform for victims to share their stories and seek help.

Her commitment to the cause goes beyond just attending events or writing statements. She has visited shelters, met with survivors, and listened to their experiences firsthand. Her deep empathy and understanding of the challenges victims face have earned her respect in the domestic abuse advocacy community. Camilla's role as a royal figure has provided her with the unique ability to amplify these voices and push for change in a way that few others can.

In 2016, Camilla helped launch the *Helpline for Domestic Violence* campaign, which sought to provide a confidential and accessible resource for individuals experiencing domestic abuse. Through her involvement in these initiatives, she has not only advocated for better services but has also worked to raise public awareness, ensuring that people know where to turn when they need help.

## Camilla's Partnerships with Charitable Organizations

Throughout her years of charitable work, Camilla has formed partnerships with numerous organizations, each of which aligns with her values and vision for creating positive social change. Her collaborations have extended across various sectors, from literacy and education to health and social welfare. These partnerships have been integral to her ability to affect meaningful change, as they provide a wider platform for her advocacy.

One notable partnership is with *The Prince's Trust*, an organization that supports young people in building their skills and confidence to help them succeed in life. Camilla's work with *The Prince's Trust* has focused on helping young people overcome the challenges they face, particularly in areas of education, employment, and personal development. Through this work, Camilla has demonstrated her commitment to creating opportunities for the younger generation to thrive and reach their potential.

Camilla's collaboration with *The Royal British Legion* also highlights her dedication to those who have served in the military. She has worked to raise awareness about the needs of veterans and their families, promoting the importance of social support systems and mental health resources for those returning from service. Her advocacy in this area underscores her commitment to ensuring that those who serve their country are not forgotten and that their sacrifices are properly acknowledged.

# Personal Stories and Reflections from Her Charity Work

Over the years, Camilla has built relationships with the individuals and communities she has supported, and her charity work has been marked by a personal commitment to making a difference. She often speaks of the deeply moving experiences that have shaped her understanding of the challenges people face and the importance of providing support.

One personal story that stands out is Camilla's involvement in a *Women's Aid* program where she visited a safe house for victims of domestic abuse. During the visit, she met with a survivor who had left an abusive relationship and was rebuilding her life. The woman shared her story with Camilla, and the encounter left a lasting impression on the Queen Consort. It was a reminder to Camilla of the courage it takes for victims to speak out and seek help, and it fueled her resolve to continue advocating for those who are voiceless.

Another moment that has resonated with Camilla was during her involvement in the *National Literacy Trust's Readathon* program, where she met children who had never had access to books before. She witnessed firsthand the joy and excitement these children felt when they picked up their first book, and it reinforced her belief in the power of reading as a transformative force in their lives.

Through these personal stories and reflections, Camilla's commitment to philanthropy is not just seen in the hours she spends attending charity events but in the meaningful connections she builds with the people she meets along the way. Her dedication to making a positive difference in the lives of others reflects her genuine care and compassion for those less fortunate.

## Legacy of Camilla's Advocacy

As Queen Consort, Camilla's philanthropic legacy is already well-established, and her ongoing commitment to social causes continues to shape her reign. From her advocacy for literacy and domestic violence to her support for young people and veterans, Camilla has proven herself to be a queen who uses her position for good. Her charitable work is a testament to her belief in the power of individuals and communities to create positive change. Through her advocacy and partnerships, she has left a lasting imprint on the causes that matter most to her, and her legacy as a philanthropist will endure long into her reign.

# Chapter 8

## Her Influence on the Royal Family

As Queen Consort, Camilla's influence on the royal family has been profound, shaping both her personal relationship with King Charles III and her role within the monarchy. Her presence has not only solidified her position beside her husband but also played a key role in redefining the monarchy for a new generation. In this chapter, we explore Camilla's relationships with other members of the royal family, her influence on the modern monarchy, and how her role as Queen Consort has contributed to a subtle yet significant shift in the monarchy's image.

# Camilla's Relationship with King Charles III: A Shared Journey

At the core of Camilla's influence on the royal family lies her relationship with King Charles III. Their bond, one that has weathered years of public scrutiny, personal challenges, and changing royal dynamics, has become a defining element of their reign. Despite the challenges they both faced in their early lives—Charles with his royal responsibilities and Camilla with her own evolving public image—their shared understanding and commitment to their roles have shaped their partnership.

Charles and Camilla's relationship is built on mutual respect and deep affection. Their bond is not only personal but also professional, as they share numerous royal duties and engagements. Camilla's presence alongside King Charles has become a symbol of stability and continuity within the monarchy. Their shared public duties, from attending state events to overseeing charitable initiatives, have highlighted their seamless teamwork and the importance of their partnership in the modern royal family.

Their public appearances together have become emblematic of a monarchy that is moving toward a more collaborative and modern future. While Charles is the King, Camilla's role as Queen Consort is one that complements and supports his, with both playing integral parts in the future of the British royal family. Camilla's influence on Charles cannot be understated—she has supported him through many public challenges, and their shared vision for the monarchy is evident in the way they approach their duties together. As a couple, they project an image of unity, grace, and respect for tradition while embracing the need for modernization.

Camilla's role as Queen Consort has allowed her to step into a leadership role in her own right. While always in support of King Charles, she has also forged her own path, balancing royal duties with her philanthropic endeavors. Her influence on the monarchy is evident not only in the public perception of their reign but also in her active participation in shaping royal policies and causes that align with their shared values.

# Shaping the Modern Monarchy: Camilla's Subtle Influence

Camilla's impact on the monarchy has been both subtle and significant. As Queen Consort, her role has helped redefine what it means to be a member of the royal family in the modern era. In many ways, Camilla has brought a sense of relatability and warmth to the monarchy, contrasting the often distant, formal image that royals were once known for. Her down-to-earth nature, combined with her poised and dignified presence, has allowed her to bridge the gap between tradition and modernity, making the monarchy more accessible to the public.

Her influence on the monarchy is not only seen in her public persona but also in the way she conducts herself behind closed doors. Camilla has played an important role in King Charles III's vision for the future of the royal family, supporting initiatives that reflect their shared values of service, philanthropy, and modernization. Her willingness to embrace contemporary issues while respecting the traditions of the monarchy has been instrumental in ensuring that the royal family remains relevant in a rapidly changing world.

One of the most important aspects of Camilla's influence is her ability to connect with the public in a genuine and meaningful way. Over the years, she has worked to reshape her own image, moving from a figure who was once regarded with skepticism to a beloved and respected Queen Consort. Her role as a mother, grandmother, and philanthropist has allowed the public to see her as someone who, while carrying out royal duties, is also deeply invested in the well-being of the nation and its citizens.

Camilla's evolution from a controversial figure to a respected member of the royal family has been instrumental in shaping the public's perception of the monarchy itself. Her presence has helped modernize the royal family's image, making it more aligned with contemporary expectations of transparency, approachability, and service. In many ways, Camilla has become a symbol of the monarchy's adaptability and resilience, showing that it is capable of evolving while maintaining the core values that have sustained it for centuries.

## Camilla's Role in Royal Events: A Subtle Shift in the Monarchy's Image

Camilla's role in royal events, both in the UK and abroad, has helped shape the monarchy's image in the 21st century. While her duties have remained largely ceremonial, her participation in these events has become an important symbol of the monarchy's evolving role in the modern world. Whether attending state banquets, official ceremonies, or diplomatic functions, Camilla's presence is a reminder that the monarchy, while steeped in history, is also adapting to meet the needs of today's society.

Her appearance at key events, such as state visits to the Commonwealth or official ceremonies with world leaders, has allowed her to showcase her diplomatic skills and her ability to represent the monarchy with poise and warmth. Camilla's role in these events is one of partnership—working alongside King Charles III to ensure that the monarchy's message is heard both at home and abroad. Together, they represent a united front, blending the royal family's tradition with a forward-thinking vision for the future.

Her presence at high-profile occasions, such as the opening of the British Parliament or commemorative events for the royal family, has marked a shift in how the monarchy is perceived. Camilla's evolving role has shown that, while the monarchy retains its formal and ceremonial responsibilities, it is also increasingly focused on being a platform for social change, charity, and public engagement. As Queen Consort, Camilla has brought a sense of relatability to royal events, making the monarchy feel more connected to the public it serves.

Perhaps one of the most notable shifts in the monarchy's image since Camilla became Queen Consort is the emphasis on the family unit. While previous royal figures were often seen as distant or detached, Camilla's role as a mother, grandmother, and wife has made the royal family feel more humanized. Her presence at family gatherings, public engagements, and charity events highlights the monarchy's focus on social issues, family, and community.

## A Subtle but Lasting Impact

As Queen Consort, Camilla's influence on the royal family has been profound. Her relationship with King Charles III has shaped not only their personal bond but also the way the monarchy functions in the modern age. Together, they have become a symbol of unity and tradition, while also embracing the changes necessary for the monarchy to remain relevant. Camilla's role in royal events, her ability to blend tradition with modernity, and her diplomatic efforts have helped to reshape the monarchy's image, ensuring its place in the 21st century.

Her influence on the royal family is not always loud or overt, but it is undeniably significant. Camilla's subtle, yet lasting impact on the monarchy has helped define the future of the British royal family. Through her leadership, her partnership with King Charles III, and her ability to connect with the public, Camilla has shown that the monarchy can adapt and evolve while staying true to its core values. As Queen Consort, she has not only found her place within the royal family but has also helped shape its future, making her one of the most influential figures in modern royal history.

# Chapter 9

# The Media and Public Perception – The Queen Who Won Over the World

Throughout her years as a public figure, Camilla, Queen Consort, has faced intense media scrutiny, and her image has undergone a remarkable transformation. Once the subject of tabloids and sensational headlines, Camilla has evolved into one of the most respected and beloved members of the royal family. This chapter takes a candid look at how the media has depicted Camilla over the years, from her early days as the "other woman" in the Charles and

Diana saga to her current role as a dignified and well-loved Queen Consort. It also explores the strategies Camilla has used to navigate media relations, repair her image, and balance her privacy with her public duties, leading to a more favorable portrayal in the press.

# From Tabloid Scrutiny to Public Redemption

When Camilla and Prince Charles's relationship first became public, it was a source of scandal and sensationalism. The media, eager to capitalize on the breakdown of Charles's marriage to Princess Diana, cast Camilla in a negative light. Tabloid headlines referred to her as the "other woman," and the public's perception of her was tainted by her involvement in the affair that led to the divorce between Charles and Diana. For many years, Camilla was vilified, and the media coverage of her life was often cruel and invasive.

In the years that followed, as Camilla and Charles's relationship became more public and they eventually married in 2005, the media's portrayal of her remained largely negative. Some sections of the press continued to focus on her role in the royal family's most controversial chapter, often framing her as the antagonist in a drama that was both personal and deeply public. This relentless scrutiny, combined with the pressure of being in the royal spotlight, made it difficult for Camilla to gain public approval.

However, as time passed, the public's view of Camilla began to shift. The British people started to see her not as the divisive figure that the media had once portrayed, but as a woman who had endured years of criticism with grace and dignity. Her public image began to change as she took on more royal duties, attended charitable events, and demonstrated her commitment to public service. With each new public appearance, she proved that she was not just the "other woman" but a devoted wife, philanthropist, and Queen Consort. Slowly but surely, the media began to shift its tone, moving away from the sensational and toward a more nuanced portrayal of her character and role.

By the time Camilla was officially crowned Queen Consort in 2022, the media had largely softened in its treatment of her. Her careful navigation of her royal duties, her public appearances, and her commitment to charity work had earned her respect from both the public and the press. Today, Camilla is seen as a beloved and dignified figure within the royal family, respected for her steadfast support of King Charles III and her dedication to various causes.

## Navigating Media Relations: A Delicate Balance

One of the key strategies Camilla employed to repair her image over the years was a deliberate and careful approach to media relations. Unlike other members of the royal family, who may have opted for more formal or distant engagements with the press, Camilla took a more personal and measured approach. She often engaged with the media directly, choosing to appear at events that highlighted her charitable work and royal duties, allowing her actions to speak louder than any tabloid headline.

Camilla's public appearances were often accompanied by efforts to humanize her image. Whether at charity events or during state visits, she demonstrated an innate ability to connect with people from all walks of life. She made an effort to appear approachable and warm, breaking down the barriers that once made her seem distant or aloof. The more the public saw her engaged in meaningful work, the more they began to understand her as a complex individual with her own sense of purpose and responsibility.

Another key strategy was Camilla's ability to maintain a careful balance between her private and public life. While she embraced her royal duties and attended public events, she also understood the importance of maintaining her privacy. In an age of social media and constant media intrusion, Camilla was able to draw a line between her personal life and her public role. She was never one to seek the limelight or indulge in unnecessary publicity. Instead, she focused on fulfilling her duties with humility and grace, which in turn helped her cultivate a more favorable public image.

Additionally, Camilla learned to embrace the media when necessary, without allowing herself to be consumed by it. She never shied away from interviews, but she was always careful to remain composed and dignified in her interactions with the press. By controlling the narrative in this way, she was able to slowly shift the public perception of her, moving from a figure of scandal to one of strength, resilience, and dedication.

# The Role of Charity Work in Shaping Her Image

One of the most effective ways Camilla improved her image in the media was through her tireless commitment to charitable work. Over the years, she became deeply involved in numerous causes, particularly those that aligned with her personal values. Her work with organizations such as the *National Literacy Trust*, *SafeLives*, and *The Prince's Trust* allowed the media to see her as a philanthropist, focused on making a tangible impact on society. By consistently championing causes such as domestic violence, literacy, and mental health, Camilla demonstrated that she was not just a royal figurehead but a woman with a genuine desire to make a difference.

Her charity work gave the media a new lens through which to view her, one that was far removed from the tabloid frenzy that once dominated her story. By being visible at charity events, engaging with the public, and using her position to amplify important causes, Camilla showed the world that she was committed to a life of service and compassion. This, more than any royal title, began to define her public image as one of a caring, approachable, and responsible figure within the royal family.

The media's portrayal of Camilla began to mirror the positive impact she was having through her charitable work. Her involvement in these causes allowed the press to see her as a woman who was not just focused on herself or her royal duties, but who was genuinely invested in improving the lives of others. This shift was pivotal in changing the media narrative about her, helping to repair her image and elevate her standing in the public eye.

# The Careful Balance of Privacy and Public Duty

One of the most significant aspects of Camilla's relationship with the media has been her ability to balance her privacy with her royal duties. The British royal family has long struggled with the tension between public and private life, with the press often intruding into personal matters. Camilla has been no exception to this, but she has learned to manage this delicate balance with grace.

While Camilla's private life has largely remained off-limits to the press, she has never completely shied away from public scrutiny. She has used her role as Queen Consort to focus on issues that matter to her, staying true to her philanthropic commitments while maintaining a level of privacy that protects her personal life. This balance has allowed her to navigate the complexities of royal life without becoming overwhelmed by the constant media attention.

By managing her personal boundaries while fulfilling her royal duties, Camilla has demonstrated that it is possible to be both a public figure and a private individual. Her ability to navigate the media while maintaining her dignity has played a major role in shifting her public perception and gaining her the respect she enjoys today.

## The Queen Who Won Over the World

Today, Camilla is widely regarded as a beloved and dignified Queen Consort, a remarkable transformation from the days when she was the target of relentless media criticism. Her ability to repair her image, navigate media relations, and balance her private life with her royal duties has been key to her successful rebranding as a compassionate, resilient, and relatable figure.

Through her charity work, her diplomatic engagement, and her steadfast support of King Charles III, Camilla has proven that she is much more than the tabloid figure she once was. The media's perception of her has evolved into one of admiration and respect, and she has firmly established herself as a Queen Consort who is dedicated to making a positive impact on the world.

Her journey from media scrutiny to public affection is a testament to her strength, patience, and ability to remain true to herself, even in the face of adversity. The Queen who once faced the world's harshest judgments is now a monarch who has won over the hearts of many, and her legacy as a beloved figure in the royal family will continue to shape the monarchy for generations to come.

# Chapter 10

## Camilla's Legacy

As Queen Consort, Camilla's legacy is already beginning to take shape. From a life that was once marked by controversy and public scrutiny, she has evolved into a beloved and respected figure in the British monarchy. Her contributions to the royal family, her influence on British society, and her personal transformation have left an indelible mark on history. This chapter reflects on the impact of her reign as Queen Consort, how she has shaped the monarchy, and how history will remember Queen Camilla in the years to come.

# The Impact of Her Reign on Future Generations

Camilla's reign as Queen Consort is still in its early stages, but the influence she has already had on the monarchy and the nation is undeniable. One of the most significant aspects of her legacy will be her impact on future generations of the British royal family. Her role as a mother and grandmother, and her ability to navigate the complexities of royal life while remaining true to herself, have set an example for younger generations.

As the wife of King Charles III, Camilla has not only played an important role in supporting her husband but has also demonstrated the evolving nature of the monarchy. The monarchy, long associated with rigid traditions, has adapted in recent years to reflect a more contemporary approach to public life. Camilla's ability to balance tradition with modernity has shown that the monarchy can remain relevant and connected to the people while respecting its history.

Her work in philanthropy, particularly her focus on literacy, domestic violence, and community well-being, has set a standard for future royals. Through her charity work, Camilla has demonstrated that royal duties are not confined to ceremonial events and public appearances but are deeply connected to social causes. She has shown that being a member of the royal family means using one's platform to affect real change, whether by supporting national causes or engaging with local communities.

Camilla's influence on her own children and grandchildren is also likely to be part of her lasting legacy. Her children, from her marriage to Andrew Parker Bowles, have grown up with a deep understanding of royal protocol and public life, but it is through her example that they will learn the importance of service, duty, and charitable engagement. Her grandchildren will grow up witnessing their grandmother's role as Queen Consort, and they will undoubtedly be inspired by her example of resilience, dignity, and compassion.

In the years to come, Camilla's role in shaping the next generation of royal figures—whether through her direct involvement or her influence on her family—will be remembered as an important part of her legacy. She has shown that being part of the royal family is not just about titles but about using one's position to make a positive difference in the world.

# Reflections on Her Contributions to the Monarchy and British Society

Camilla's contributions to the monarchy have been nothing short of transformative. When she first married Prince Charles, she was often regarded as a controversial figure, primarily due to her relationship with him during his marriage to Princess Diana. But over the years, she has proven herself to be a dedicated and capable member of the royal family, playing an instrumental role in supporting King Charles III and modernizing the image of the monarchy.

Her steady support of King Charles III has allowed him to take on the responsibilities of monarch with confidence, knowing that Camilla is by his side, fulfilling her duties as Queen Consort. Together, they have forged a partnership that represents both continuity and change. While Camilla has embraced the royal traditions and protocol that come with her position, she has also brought a more modern sensibility to the monarchy, helping it adapt to the needs of today's society.

One of her most significant contributions has been her philanthropic work. Camilla has championed numerous causes over the years, including literacy, domestic violence, cancer research, and mental health. Her advocacy for domestic abuse victims has been particularly notable, as she has used her platform to raise awareness about the issue and support initiatives aimed at helping survivors. Through her charity work, Camilla has shown that the monarchy's role extends beyond ceremonial duties and has a real impact on the lives of ordinary people.

In British society, Camilla's contributions have helped shift the perception of the royal family. She has demonstrated that royalty is not just about pomp and circumstance, but about serving the public and engaging with important social issues. Her ability to balance her royal duties with her personal values has earned her the respect of the public, and her efforts to bring attention to critical issues have further cemented her place as a respected figure in British society.

Camilla's quiet, steady presence in the royal family has also served as a stabilizing force during times of change. As King Charles III ascended to the throne following the death of Queen Elizabeth II, Camilla played a key role in ensuring a smooth transition, helping to maintain continuity within the monarchy while also signaling a new era. In this sense, her contributions to the monarchy have been not only significant but also essential to its future success.

# Speculations on How History Will Remember Queen Camilla

As with any public figure, history will ultimately decide how Queen Camilla is remembered. However, based on her actions and the way she has handled her royal duties, it seems likely that she will be remembered as a Queen Consort who played a pivotal role in shaping the modern monarchy.

Camilla's legacy will likely be one of transformation. She has successfully navigated the challenges of public life, moving from being a controversial figure to one of the most respected members of the royal family. Her work with various charities, her efforts to modernize the monarchy, and her unwavering support for her husband, King Charles III, will be among the defining aspects of her reign as Queen Consort.

In years to come, historians may look back on Camilla's role as a model for future consorts. Her ability to balance tradition with modernity, her compassion for the causes she champions, and her dedication to her royal duties will likely be viewed as key factors in her success. Her personal growth and resilience, overcoming early public skepticism to become one of the most beloved royals, will surely be part of the story that is told.

While Camilla's legacy is still being written, it is clear that she has already left a lasting impact on the British royal family. Her contributions to the monarchy, her advocacy for important social issues, and her partnership with King Charles III will ensure that her place in history is a significant one. As Queen Consort, Camilla has proven that even in a modern monarchy, tradition and progress can go hand in hand, and her legacy will serve as a testament to the strength, dignity, and compassion that define her reign.

# Conclusion

Camilla's journey from a controversial figure to a beloved royal is nothing short of remarkable. When she first came into the public eye as the woman involved in the breakdown of Prince Charles's marriage to Princess Diana, the media's portrayal of her was overwhelmingly negative. She was often vilified, scrutinized, and cast as the antagonist in a royal drama that captivated the world. Yet, through years of public service, personal growth, and steadfast dedication to her royal duties, Camilla has evolved into a respected and admired Queen Consort. Her story is one of resilience, transformation, and unwavering commitment to both the royal family and the British public.

As Queen Consort, Camilla has not only supported King Charles III in his role as monarch but has also carved out her own space within the monarchy. Her contributions to charitable causes, her efforts to modernize the royal image, and her ability to balance tradition with modern sensibilities have helped reshape the public's perception of the monarchy. Today, she is seen as a dignified, compassionate, and capable queen who plays an integral role in the future of the royal family.

Camilla's evolving public image is a testament to her ability to navigate the complexities of royal life with grace and authenticity. Her early years in the public eye were fraught with controversy, but she gradually won over both the media and the British public. Through her involvement in various charitable causes, her calm and steady presence beside King Charles, and her refusal to be defined by past scandals, she has become a beloved figure in the royal family. Camilla has demonstrated that even in the face of adversity, one can remain true to their values and grow into a role of great responsibility.

As we look to the future of the British royal family, Camilla's place as Queen Consort is secure. Her partnership with King Charles III, built on mutual respect and shared values, is poised to shape the monarchy for years to come. Her role will continue to be one of influence, both in supporting her husband's reign and in her own right as a champion of important causes. In the years ahead, as the monarchy faces new challenges and continues to evolve, Camilla's contributions will be a guiding force, ensuring that the royal family remains connected to the people it serves.

In reflecting on her legacy, it is clear that Camilla's journey is far from over. While she has already secured her place in history as a pivotal figure in the monarchy's modern evolution, her influence will continue to resonate in the years to come. As Queen Consort, she has proven that the monarchy can embrace change while staying rooted in tradition, and her legacy will undoubtedly be one of positive transformation, compassion, and service to the people of the United Kingdom and the Commonwealth.

Printed in Great Britain
by Amazon